IMAGES OF WAR

THE GERMAN SIEGE OF LENINGRAD 1941–1944

RARE PHOTOGRAPHS FROM WARTIME ARCHIVES

Ian Baxter

Pen & Sword
MILITARY

First published in Great Britain in 2023 by
PEN & SWORD MILITARY
an imprint of Pen & Sword Books Ltd
Yorkshire – Philadelphia

ISBN 978-1-39906-466-8

Typeset by Concept, Huddersfield, West Yorkshire, HD4 5JL.
Printed and bound in England by CPI Group (UK) Ltd, Croydon, CR0 4YY.

MIX
Paper | Supporting
responsible forestry
FSC
www.fsc.org
FSC® C013604

Pen & Sword Books Ltd incorporates the imprints of After the Battle, Aviation, Atlas, Family History, Fiction, Maritime, Military, Discovery, Politics, History, Archaeology, Select, Wharncliffe Local History, Wharncliffe True Crime, Military Classics, Wharncliffe Transport, Leo Cooper, The Praetorian Press, Remember When, White Owl, Seaforth Publishing and Frontline Books.

For a complete list of Pen & Sword titles please contact
PEN & SWORD BOOKS LTD
47 Church Street, Barnsley, South Yorkshire, S70 2AS, England
E-mail: enquiries@pen-and-sword.co.uk
Website: www.pen-and-sword.co.uk
or
PEN & SWORD BOOKS
1950 Lawrence Rd, Havertown, PA 19083, USA
E-mail: uspen-and-sword@casematepublishers.com
Website: www.penandswordbooks.com

Contents

About the Author

Ian Baxter is a military historian who specializes in German twentieth-century military history. He has written more than fifty books including *Poland – The Eighteen Day Victory March*, *Panzers In North Africa*, *The Ardennes Offensive*, *The Western Campaign*, *The 12th SS Panzer-Division Hitlerjugend*, *The Waffen-SS on the Western Front*, *The Waffen-SS on the Eastern Front*, *The Red Army at Stalingrad*, *Elite German Forces of World War II*, *Armoured Warfare*, *German Tanks of War*, *Blitzkrieg*, *Panzer-Divisions at War 1939–1945*, *Hitler's Panzers*, *German Armoured Vehicles of World War Two*, *Last Two Years of the Waffen-SS at War*, *German Soldier Uniforms and Insignia*, *German Guns of the Third Reich*, *Defeat to Retreat: The Last Years of the German Army At War 1943–45*, *Operation Bagration – the Destruction of Army Group Centre*, *German Guns of the Third Reich*, *Rommel and the Afrika Korps*, *U-Boat War*, and most recently *The Sixth Army and the Road to Stalingrad*. He has written over a hundred articles including 'Last days of Hitler', 'Wolf's Lair', 'The Story of the V1 and V2 Rocket Programme', 'Secret Aircraft of World War Two', 'Rommel at Tobruk', 'Hitler's War With his Generals', 'Secret British Plans to Assassinate Hitler', 'The SS at Arnhem', 'Hitlerjugend', 'Battle of Caen 1944', 'Gebirgsjäger at War', 'Panzer Crews', 'Hitlerjugend Guerrillas', 'Last Battles in the East', 'The Battle of Berlin', and many more. He has also reviewed numerous military studies for publication, supplied thousands of photographs and important documents to various publishers and film production companies worldwide, and lectures to various schools, colleges and universities throughout the United Kingdom and Southern Ireland.

Introduction

The siege of Leningrad was a prolonged military blockade undertaken by the German war machine, Army Group North, on the Eastern Front. Drawing on a superb collection of rare and unpublished photographs together with detailed captions and text, this dramatic book describes the 872-day siege that began in earnest on 8 September 1941 and did not lift until 27 January 1944. It shows the Wehrmacht forces that surrounded Leningrad, including the many various artillery units that constantly bombarded the city.

During the course of the siege it details the various attempts by the Red Army to break the blockade and shows German forces together with their Spanish and Finnish allies doggedly resisting the attacks. Eventually, due to overwhelming enemy pressure, the Germans were forced to retreat, but not before looting and destroying a number of historical palaces and landmarks and stealing a large number of valuable art collections.

The German siege became one of the longest and most destructive blockades in military history, which not only saw thousands of soldiers killed during fighting to resist and unblock the city but also saw the systematic starvation of the population trapped inside and the intentional destruction of its buildings.

Chapter One

Objective Leningrad 1941

At dawn on 22 June 1941, along a 1,800-mile-long invasion front, 3 million German soldiers on the frontier of the Soviet Union unleashed one of the most brutal conflicts of the twentieth century: Operation BARBAROSSA. Directing this invasion of Russia were Field Marshal Ritter von Leeb, commander of Army Group North, Field Marshal Fedor von Bock in the centre and Field Marshal von Rundstedt in the south. Von Leeb's Army Group North was given the task of destroying the Red Army fighting in the Baltic region. Hitler stipulated on the eve of the invasion that the German objective was to thrust across East Prussia, smashing Soviet positions along the Baltic, liquidating the bases of the Baltic Fleet, destroying what was left of Russian naval power and capturing Kronstadt and Leningrad. Once the city had been razed to the ground, the German armies could sweep down from the north while the main force closed in from the west. With 500,000 men at von Leeb's disposal comprising almost thirty divisions, six of them armoured and motorized with 1,500 Panzers and 12,000 heavy weapons, plus an aviation fleet of almost 1,000 aircraft, he was determined to strike along the Baltic coast and dispose of the Russian force once and for all.

Von Leeb's rapid two-pronged offensive along the Baltic opened up at first light on 22 June 1941. His force, consisting of the 16th and 18th Armies, smashed through the Soviet defences. Russian soldiers stood helpless in its path, too shocked to take action. During coming weeks, Army Group North continued to chew through enemy positions heading through Lithuania, Latvia and Estonia, towards their objective of Leningrad. Hitler had told von Leeb in no uncertain terms that 'Leningrad and Moscow must be razed and made uninhabitable. Otherwise the population will have to be fed during the winter. The Luftwaffe will raze them. The nest of Bolshevism must be destroyed. That will be a national disaster for the Russians.' Von Leeb assured his Führer that he would have forced Leningrad's capitulation by 21 July 1941. 'So far as I am concerned, Führer, Leningrad is already a city of death and despair.'

For Hitler the city of Leningrad held a strange fascination; a preoccupation that never left his thoughts. To him the city was a 'Red incubator' of an ideology against which he was leading a crusade. He saw the Russian city not only as the birth of revolutionary Communism but as St Petersburg, a fortress city built by Peter I for his conquest of the Baltic. For centuries the Germans had regarded the Baltic Sea as their sea, and now in 1941 Hitler was determined to rewrite history and claim it. 'Leningrad,' he said, 'must be captured; the Baltic secured; Soviet naval power must be destroyed; Kronstadt must be levelled. Then – and only then – would an assault on Moscow begin.'

Von Leeb's offensive on Leningrad was rapid. Fortunately for the Germans, the earth was baked hard by the blistering summer heat and the troops, together with their armoured columns, were able to advance rapidly through the Baltics. Everything appeared to go well and German commanders, even veteran ones like von Manstein, marvelled at the speed of the advance. The military progress on the road to Leningrad gave Hitler every reason to celebrate his triumph of strategy and arms in the East.

By 10 July, von Leeb's units broke south of Pskov and rolled towards Luga. At the rate they were advancing they would need no more than nine or ten days to reach the outskirts of Leningrad, but following their initial surge of success, the Wehrmacht was losing momentum. Not only were their supply lines being overstretched, but enemy resistance began to stiffen on the road to Leningrad. In a desperate attempt to blunt the German advance and prevent them from reaching the imperial city, brigades of Russian Marines, naval units and more than 80,000 men from the Baltic Fleet were hastily sent into action against von Leeb's forces. These Russian soldiers were now the sole barrier between Leningrad and the Germans. Although the advance was hampered by these Russian forces that delayed the Germans by six weeks, by the end of August 1941 von Leeb's Panzers were finally within sight of Leningrad. The terrified civilians left inside the city walls were then about to endure one of the most brutal sieges in twentieth-century history.

As the summer of 1941 passed and the Germans drew closer to the city gates, Leningraders were given the grim orders to defend their city to the death. Although von Leeb's forces had arrived within shelling distance of Leningrad, the advance had not gone as planned. Already units had been badly disrupted and were mired on the Leningrad Front by stiffening resistance. Even von Leeb himself was by then under considerable pressure from Hitler to complete his assignment of encircling Leningrad, to join forces with the Finns and to wipe out the Baltic Fleet. His forces were desperately needed for the Moscow Front, where the Wehrmacht were preparing to go in for the kill and capture the capital. Yet despite assurances from von Leeb that his forces were making good progress, German troops were still entangled in hundreds of miles of earth walls, anti-tank ditches and wire barricades, thousands of defensive pillboxes and the harrying activities of Russian tanks outside Leningrad.

By 17 September, the Moscow Front could wait no longer for victory in the north. The shift of the main weight, the powerful 41st Panzer Corps required by von Leeb to sledgehammer his way to the outskirts of Leningrad, was taken out of line and ordered to the Moscow Front. Without the 41st Panzer Corps the whole dynamic of Army Group North had altered. There would now be no attack on Leningrad. Instead, Hitler ordered that the city be encircled and the inhabitants defending inside would be starved to death. By October and November 1941, some ten German divisions were tied down around the city.

Opening attacks in Northern Russia. Along the Baltic German forces attacked at first light on the morning of 22 June 1941. Both the German 16th and 18th Armies smashed through the Soviet defences to begin their advance towards Leningrad. For the German soldier Russia proved to be a totally alien environment. The vast open spaces, with endless horizons and lack of landmarks for guidance, were a constant problem for the Landseer. In the summer months of 1941, in spite of the successful advance by Army Group North, the soldiers complained bitterly about the vast distances and the inadequate road system.

German troops advancing across into the Baltics to begin their first enemy contact. The main manoeuvre elements of the infantry regiments were of course to fire and gain as much ground as possible and then hold the position. Normally two regiments would be deployed forward with one in reserve. However, it was not uncommon, especially following a few weeks of fighting where the front coverage was so extensive, that all three regiments were inserted in the front line.

A photograph taken following the aftermath of a German attack along a road. Dead horses are strewn along the roadside intermingled with the burned-out remains of Russian vehicles.

An interesting photograph showing a column of PaK 35/36s being towed by animal draught along a road during the advance towards Leningrad in the summer of 1941. This particular weapon was the standard anti-tank gun of the Landseer during the early part of the war. It weighed only 432kg (952.5lb) and had a sloping splinter shield. The gun fired a solid-shot round at a muzzle velocity of 762m/s (2,500 ft/s) to a maximum range of 4,025m (13,200ft).

(**Opposite, above**) Horse-drawn infantry pass a destroyed Russian artillery piece. Both the 16th and 18th Armies rapidly smashed through the Soviet defences and decimated their lines. During the coming weeks Army Group North advanced at breakneck speed through Lithuania, Latvia and Estonia, straight towards their objective of Leningrad. Fortunately for the Germans, the earth had become baked by the blistering summer heat and von Leeb's army was able to advance rapidly through the Baltic States.

(**Opposite, below**) A column of infantry on horseback. Although the infantry regiments were supplied with light trucks to move ordnance and other equipment to the front, many infantry regiments, especially those recently-raised divisions, relied heavily on horses. Motorized prime movers were preferred as it was necessary to rapidly move weapons and supplies from position to position in order to survive and effectively engage the enemy.

(**Above**) A light Horch vehicle together with a support truck crosses a prefabricated bridge bound for the front.

Two photographs showing officers conferring with the aid of maps about the next operational move on the central front. Within the first couple of weeks of the lightning strike against the bewildered Russian force, Army Group North was advancing at speed towards their main objective, the city of Leningrad. Yet, despite this success, by the first week of July commanders were deeply concerned about maintaining the momentum due to the bad road system, rain and the increased length of their supply lines.

(**Above**) A variety of vehicles advance along a congested road. Motorcycles, support vehicles and a column of infantry vehicles can be seen here. Note that each infantry vehicle possesses a bipod mount with an attached MG 34 machine gun. Support vehicles were often issued with light machine guns for self-defence and a lightweight anti-aircraft tripod 34.

(**Opposite, above**) The distances over which these troops marched were immense. Whenever possible, short breaks usually consisted of getting as much as sleep as possible or resting and eating, for they knew that once they reached their objective there was a good prospect of heavy contact with Soviet formations. Note the mobile field kitchen or 'Goulash Cannon' set-up. This vehicle was officially known as a Hf.12 (*Heeresfeldwagen*) kitchen wagon. These small mobile kitchens could also operate on the move, cooking stews, soups and making coffee. The limber carried utensils and equipment and was often towed by animal draught.

(**Opposite, below**) To overcome the perils of traffic movement, pioneer troops are seen here laying felled pine trees to provide an adequate road system for the vehicles to pass over. This type of improvised road-building was primarily undertaken on sodden ground in order to support the weight of tanks, heavy artillery and other equipment destined for the front lines. A common occurrence on the Eastern Front, even during the summer months, was heavy rain. Motor vehicles often struggled along the dirt roads after heavy rainfall and turned the dusty rutted roads into mud. As a result of heavy traffic the dirt roads were constantly being churned up and created even greater problems for the vehicles following in the rear.

A popular mode of transport with the Wehrmacht throughout the war was the bicycle. Here soldiers negotiate an uneven road on their bicycles and occasionally halt for a respite. The march through northern Russia was long and arduous, for both men and animals. This photograph gives an excellent picture of a typical infantryman's combat equipment. The men are equipped with a gas mask canister, gas mask cape and rifle ammunition pouches for their Karabiner 98k rifle. Attached to their belts are their M35 steel helmets painted in a rough texture matt slate-grey.

A long column of animal draught towing 10.5cm howitzers towards the front. Although these howitzers provided armour-piercing and shaped-charge anti-tank rounds, the guns were far from being effective anti-tank weapons. An average artillery regiment was equipped with some 2,500 troops and 2,274 horses, the latter drawing more than 200 wagons and artillery caissons. With so many horses being utilized, a high percentage was often killed in action as a result. The 10.5cm howitzer was primarily given the task of destroying enemy positions and fortified defences and conducting counter-battery fire prior to an armoured or infantry assault.

Infantry shown marching forward towards the front. A typical infantry division consisted of three infantry regiments, an artillery regiment, reconnaissance, anti-tank, pioneer and signal battalions, plus divisional services. Trucks, animal draught with their caisson transported much of the supporting battalions, but there were many infantry that marched on foot including all the supply columns that were horse-drawn.

(**Above**) A long column of horse-drawn transport is seen here advancing along a road bound for the front. Note the 15cm howitzer being towed by animal draught. The gun was broken down into two loads, each drawn by six horses. The gun's tube and breech were transported on a special four-wheeled wagon.

(**Opposite, above**) A motorcyclist wearing the standard motorcyclist's rubberized waterproof coat can be seen here in a village surrounded by locals. This soldier probably belongs to a motorcyclist messenger platoon. Such a platoon was a vital asset to the divisional staff and enabled the officers and staff to receive and dispatch vital information on the battlefield. Motorcyclists were also utilized for reconnaissance duties. Because they were very versatile machines, they enabled the rider to survey enemy positions until he encountered fire and then return swiftly with important data and other information relating to the location and strength of the enemy.

(**Opposite, below**) The first of nine photographs showing Russian PoWs captured during Army Group North's powerful drive through the Baltic States in the summer of 1941. Although Nazi propaganda portrayed the Russian soldier and his nation as subhuman, during the early days of Operation BARBAROSSA the average German soldier treated their enemy relatively well. However, generally German infantry were indoctrinated to hate their enemy, and on the battlefield they smashed through the Soviet lines attempting to kill as many of the enemy as possible without taking prisoners. These soldiers would have been escorted to the rear and their fate can only be imagined. Many of them during this early stage of the war were sent directly to holding areas. However, as the numbers of prisoners increased, many were sent on to labour or concentration camps, or simply taken away and executed.

A 21cm Möser 18 being readied for transportation. This powerful long-range counter-battery gun was mounted in a 'mortar-style' carriage that allowed very high elevation. The weapon was part of the 21cm Mörser-Abt. (mot.). It proved to be one of the best heavy guns in service in 1941 and had an impressive range, but it was never a common weapon.

Bound for Leningrad, a column of armoured vehicles can be seen here advancing along a road. A prime mover is towing a 15cm heavy field howitzer. This particular gun was primarily designed to attack targets deeper in the enemy's rear. This included command posts, reserve units, assembly areas and logistics facilities.

(**Opposite, above**) Infantry, support vehicles and animal draught towing supplies pouring across a prefabricated bridge. The majority of the support elements, as well as artillery, supply and transport were horse-drawn. Some elements were motorized or partly motorized, especially the headquarters, reconnaissance, anti-tank, engineer and signals units.

(**Opposite, below**) A battery of 15cm field howitzers has been set up here on the edge of a wooded area in preparation for a fire mission against an enemy target. This weapon was the standard piece in a division and employment of artillery was a necessity to any ground force engaging an enemy. Both infantry and motorized artillery regiments became the backbone of the fighting in the early years of the war.

(**Above**) One of the most difficult aspects of travelling through Russia by wheeled vehicle was the terrible road network. Often just a short shower of rain could turn a relatively normal tract of land or dusty road into a sea of mud. Consequently this made moving from one part of the front to another very hard going. Here in this photograph animal draught is shown struggling to tow ordnance through the mire. Much of the march with animal draught was often undertaken on foot to reduce the load's weight in the snow, mud or on rough ground. The crew also had to assist by pushing. During the autumn and winter period, much of the movement of wheeled vehicles consisted of many hours of digging them out or trying to make the roads passable for the never-ending stream of military traffic.

(**Above**) Across uneven muddy ground support services and artillerymen struggle with the unit's artillery limber and caisson. Often crewmen riding on the caisson and limber would have to follow on foot to reduce the load's weight in the mud and on rough ground. The mud produced from just a few hours of rain in Russia was enough to immobilize whole columns of wheeled transport including tanks.

(**Opposite**) Two photographs showing a typical road network in northern Russia during the early autumn of 1941. The all-weather roads had not then been constructed to carry the numbers and weight of traffic that now use them and the surfaces began to break up under the strain. The roads shown here have been reduced to a mud track. In these conditions, horses were often used but hundreds of them died from heart strain brought on by their efforts to haul the heavy loads of stranded vehicles or artillery pieces through the mud. These 15cm howitzers would be used for bombing Russian positions around Leningrad. The power of these heavy field guns could hurl their destructive charge almost 9 miles into the enemy lines. The 15cm gun was normally broken down into two loads, each drawn by six horses. Although the 15cm howitzer proved a success against enemy targets during the siege of Leningrad, crews found the weapon too heavy. By 1943 only a few of these guns remained in active service and were used mainly in Russia until the end of the war.

Here a German unit has reached the outskirts of Leningrad and buildings are on fire following heavy ground and aerial bombardments.

Two German motorcyclists pose for the camera with a stuffed Russian bear and a makeshift sign during their advance on the city of Leningrad. Note the captured Russian Army helmet on the bear's head and the animal clutching a beer in celebration.

Chapter Two

Leningrad Defences

For almost three months the inhabitants of the city of Leningrad had been preparing themselves for the inevitable arrival of the German forces. Most believed that the Germans intended to either raze or occupy the city, and those left alive in the smouldering remains were either to be dragged off to a labour camp or shot. Yet whatever their fate, each civilian worry was compounded into one single thought of survival.

Just days after Molotov's famous broadcast to the Russian nation giving them shocking news of the German invasion, the inhabitants of Leningrad began the grim task of preparing their own city for war. At first nothing more than protecting buildings with sandbags, the digging of slit trenches and the construction of makeshift air-raid shelters was undertaken, but as the German advance gathered momentum and the audible crump of heavy enemy artillery began drawing closer each day, groups of men and women found them being pressed into defence gangs. Thousands of people assembled in the city's parks, squares and gardens, and were fitted out with an assortment of various crude tools. They were then marched or transported in packed trains and vehicles to sites some miles outside Leningrad for defence duties.

Frantically, especially west of the city where the enemy was expected to approach, almost 300,000 soldiers, defence gangs and a high proportion of teenage children stretching a distance of almost 100 miles erected pillboxes, dug anti-tank ditches and laid miles of anti-tank obstacles. At the same time, closer to the city, a number of concentric rings of defences were constructed at remarkable speed. All over the city the defenders, compelled by desperation, built roadblocks and crude defence barriers. There were masses of steel anti-tank obstacles and old vehicles including disguised tram cars filled with stones.

In addition to the massive defence of Leningrad, some 200,000 men and women came flocking at first as volunteers in what was called the 'People's Army'. Factory workers, small shop-keepers and petty officials were all recruited. Even physically disabled people that were not suitable for defensive combat enlisted. Although completely untrained with no military experience, almost every 'Soviet comrade' in the new 'People's Army' was willing to defend their city. Even the commander of the city garrison, Lieutenant General Popov, was quite willing to send, without any type of training, thousands of men and women to the front lines. Even those that had no weapons were instructed to harass the enemy 'by such means as throwing boiling water at enemy troops, or attempting to encircle groups of German soldiers with burning rings of kerosene.'

As the summer of 1941 passed and German forces approached the gates of Leningrad, the city's inhabitants were given a proclamation to defend to the death:

> Comrades. Leningraders! Dear Friends! Our dearly beloved city is in imminent danger of attack … the Red Army is striving valiantly to defend the approaches to our city … but the enemy has not yet been crushed, his resources are not yet exhausted … he wants to smash all our homes, our families, honour and freedom.

However, behind this patriotic proclamation stood harsh measures designed to warn anyone of the terrible consequences of failing in their duty to the 'Motherland'. Stalin himself had declared that all those who surrendered to the enemy, regardless of circumstances, would be treated as deserters and subsequently executed. A personal order went out to soldiers on the Leningrad Front warning them not to retreat one inch. The Military Council of Leningrad warned:

> All traitors who try to commit treasonable acts, hold conversation with the enemy, or desert to the other side are to be fired upon without warning and destroyed by any available means. The commanders and commissars of the units in which treasonable 'fraternization' and treason to our country are to be arrested and turned over to the military tribunals … All soldiers of this front are to be informed that everyone who fails to take action against the traitors and criminals, lets them escape, or reveals cowardice and disorder in such cases is to be mercilessly destroyed as a helper of the fascist master.

Ten days later following the proclamation on 1 September 1941, the first German shell fell upon the city. The siege of Leningrad had begun.

(**Opposite, above**) Civilians working on the Luga defensive line in the summer of 1941. This defence line ran almost 200 miles in length from the Gulf of Finland along the Rivers Luga, Mshaga and Luga Shelon to Lake Ilmen. Construction of the defensive line began in early July 1941 when strong German spearheads began breaking through south of Lake Peipus. In order to try to hold back the German advance, Red Army troops comprising the Luga Operational Group, the Leningrad Infantry School, the Kingisepp Militia and the Leningrad Gun and MG Infantry School concentrated in the area east of the city of Narva. A separate mountain rifle brigade recruited from Leningrad supported the Luga Operational Group by defending the Luga line.

(**Opposite, below**) Russian civilians digging a defensive position in front of Leningrad in 1941, probably the Luga line. The creation and defence of this line was assigned to *General Leytenant* Konstantin Piadyshev who commanded the Luga Operational Group. It comprised, from north to south, the 191st, 111th and 177th divisions supported by the 3rd Tank Division and the 1st Mountain Brigade together with other formations of the Northern Front.

(**Above**) Another image showing Russian civilians digging along the Luga line. This line was of paramount importance to the defence of Leningrad and was held long enough to thwart the Germans from launching a direct assault.

(**Opposite, above**) Decorated Russian soldiers – probably from the Luga Operational Group – standing next to civilians who assisted in working on the Luga defensive line during the summer of 1941. Behind the Luga line some 1 million civilians were used to construct fortifications on the north and south sides of the city and various other lines of defence around the perimeter. Many of the civilians were often ruthlessly conscripted into gangs to dig vast anti-tank trenches.

(**Opposite, below**) An anti-aircraft gun can be seen here in action during a night-time raid on the city of Leningrad in the summer of 1941. As the German 4th Panzer Group reached the Luga line on 12 July 1941, German bombers pounded the line and heavily attacked the city, launching both day and night-time attacks.

Anti-aircraft guns can be seen here defending the skies in front of St Isaac's Cathedral in Leningrad. In order to try to prevent the cathedral being bombed by enemy aircraft, the dome was painted over in grey. In the building's skylight a geodesic intersection point was erected to calculate the location and position of German artillery batteries.

The first two images show Soviet barrage balloons being transported along Nevsky Prospekt in Leningrad on 9 October 1941. The other photograph shows barrage balloons being moved along a road in front of St Isaac's Cathedral. Numerous balloons were positioned in the city to minimize low-flying enemy aircraft attacks. Some of these balloons carried small explosive charges that would be pulled up against the aircraft to ensure its destruction. German dive-bombers were very vulnerable, but the balloons had little effect against high-flying German bombers. The Luftwaffe was determined to systematically bombard both the civilian and military infrastructure in an attempt to crush the morale of the Leningraders.

(**Opposite, above**) Soldiers hauling a camouflaged artillery gun along a typical muddy road during defensive operations in front of Leningrad in late 1941. The defence of Leningrad was extensive with more than 500 miles of anti-tank ditches and wire obstacles, 15,000 pillboxes and bunkers, 22,000 firing points and 2,300 command and observation posts deployed on the approaches to the city.

(**Opposite, below**) During an enemy contact in late 1941 on the outskirts of the city near the old Detskoe Selo train Soviet machine-gunners can be seen armed with their Pulemyot Maxima PM1910 (PM M1910). Note the large armoured shield that was mounted over the gun's jacketed barrel. This protected the gunner from incoming small-arms fire and artillery fragmentation. However, the drawback of the shield was that it made the weapon very heavy to manoeuvre and a target for the enemy. As a consequence Russian soldiers often removed the shield, especially in close-quarter or urbanized fighting.

(**Above**) An 85mm air defence gun M1939 (52-K) in an elevated position in preparation for a fire mission against enemy aircraft. Camouflaged netting can be seen concealing the weapon. This gun was successfully used throughout the war on the Eastern Front against bombers and other high- and medium-altitude targets. In emergencies these guns were used as powerful anti-tank weapons. The 85mm M1939 gun was organized into heavy anti-aircraft regiments of sixteen guns. The regiments were organized into divisions of the field anti-aircraft forces.

(**Above**) Russian troops operating outside the city in late 1941. Note the soldier armed with the PTRS-41 or Simonov anti-tank rifle. This weapon fired a 14.5mm armour-piercing bullet with a muzzle velocity of 1,013m/s and devastating ballistics. It could penetrate armour plate of up to 40mm thickness to a distance of 100 metres.

(**Opposite**) Soviet troops of the 168th Infantry Division in a trench during defensive operations outside Leningrad in late 1941.

(**Below**) Russian naval infantrymen manning a machine-gun position during winter operations in 1942 near the Gulf of Finland outside Leningrad.

(**Above**) Civilians can be seen here clearing rubble along a Leningrad street. German Army Group North continued its advance on Leningrad until late September 1941, when Russian forces halted them in the suburbs of the city. With German forces now stagnated outside the city along trenches, Hitler changed strategy and ordered his force to prepare Leningrad for a siege. He was determined to erase the city from the face of the earth by encircling it and levelling it to the ground by means of artillery bombardment and continual bombing from the air.

(**Opposite**) During surveillance duties from an observation post two Russian women can be seen here on air defence duties, surveying the skies and enemy ground positions outside Leningrad.

(**Above**) Defenders of Leningrad: workers of the Kirov Factory greeting young sailors on a bridge during the siege.

(**Opposite**) Russian soldiers marching through the city towards the front to undertake defensive operations.

(**Below**) A Russian tank can be seen here knocked out of action on the outskirts of Leningrad. A German infantryman is seen walking from a destroyed building towards the knocked-out vehicle.

A young Russian boy soldier captured during defensive fighting on the outskirts of Leningrad. There were even children as young as 12 that were recruited into some units to defend the city. In some cases, orphans also unofficially joined the Soviet Red Army.

Chapter Three

The Siege

After the first German shell landed on the city, eight days later Leningrad was once again hit but this time with hundreds of shells. This would be the first of a series of heavy artillery bombardments coupled with hundreds of Luftwaffe sorties. Many houses were destroyed and several warehouses were razed including food production plants deliberately bombed. Most Leningraders had already taken to their cellars, air-raid shelters and bunkers for they now feared a main German attack into the city. Outside Leningrad hard-pressed Russian soldiers were desperately trying to hold their defensive lines and prevent forward German units making contact with Finnish forces. The pulverizing effects of German armour and artillery had ground many units into a depleted and exhausted band of discouraged men. The death toll had become so bad that the Germans reported many hundreds of Russian troops deserting. Signs of disintegration plagued every sector of the front, but still hundreds more Russian soldiers replaced those that fell in front of German gunfire. A German commander noted that:

> The German military leadership is constantly amazed by the toughness and stubbornness of the Russians as well as their ability to form new troop units … Although the combat value and morale of the 'improvised' units is low, the Red Army soldiers and Leningrad workers fight as before with stolid persistence. Without changing anything in the desperate situation of Leningrad, [the Russians] nevertheless are tying down ten German divisions in the encirclement and preventing their use in other sectors of the front.

At the same time out in the Gulf of Finland the Luftwaffe attacked for days to destroy the Russian Baltic Fleet, including heavy strikes against its isolated naval garrisons on the Moonzund Peninsula, the Ösel and Kotlin islands. From Kronstadt on the island of Kotlin the Germans bombed day and night. The inhabitants of the islands were also bombed from the air, and on some days more than 200 aircraft at a time pulverized Kronstadt. Strategically Kronstadt was vital to the defence of Leningrad and the Germans attempted numerous times to destroy the island's strong artillery positions and naval batteries. German troops had captured a strip of coast some 15 miles from Peterhof to the south-western outskirts of Leningrad, but suffered severe losses from these long-range naval batteries and artillery. A Russian scout found a notebook from a dead German corporal, Hermann Fuchs, who had been killed while fighting on the edge of Leningrad:

> Yesterday and today here outside Petersburg it has been hell again. Yesterday we attacked a giant line of fortifications. Artillery fired the whole day with cases. The fire was so heavy you couldn't make out the bursts. Now again the hell has begun. In the harbour there are still one battleship and some cruisers. It is hard to describe the craters which their shells make. One burst 200 metres from me. I can say that I was thrown 2 metres into the air. I wanted to believe   and couldn't believe – that I was whole and not hurt. Because I could see the whole area covered with craters I knew that I was alive. All around me rolled parts of bodies – here a hand, there a leg, there a head.

During October and November 1941 fighting continued on the outskirts of Leningrad with unabated ferocity. Soldiers of the Leningrad Front were fighting for survival within a huge encircling ring, and the Baltic Fleet had now been squeezed into a small corner of the Gulf of Finland and repeatedly bombed by the Luftwaffe. Delivery of vital supplies for the inhabitants of the city, the soldiers at the front and the Baltic Fleet had virtually stopped. The only lifeline was a narrow strip across Lake Ladoga that had not yet been cut off by the Germans, but even this route was perilously close to the battles that raged around the city and was almost daily exposed to the terrifying enemy artillery and aerial bombardments.

Despite the dangers, the Leningraders, those that helped defend the city and those that died supplying it, fought on doggedly. Much of the city and the surrounding areas had been heavily and continuously bombed with thousands of dwellings obliterated. When the snow arrived in autumn 1941 most of the cruellest injuries of the city were concealed by snowdrifts. The freezing temperatures had a terrible effect on the population of Leningrad, with thousands of people dying as a result. The city was now beginning to feel the full effects of the German blockade. In fact, the economic destruction and human losses in Leningrad on both sides exceeded those of the Battle of Moscow and the Battle of Stalingrad. All domestic coal and fuel had been consumed and supplies of other vital materials were fast running out. As a result, cold and starvation gripped the city. Deaths peaked between January and February 1942 at a rate of 100,000 per month, mostly from starvation. Leningraders often collapsed and died on the streets, while others resorted to cannibalism to stay alive. The old, women and children regularly became frostbitten with many suffering from malnutrition or dysentery. Frequently they would be seen trudging across the blitzed snow-covered city scavenging bombed-out buildings for firewood. Repeatedly they came across the frozen corpses of people caught hiding from enemy shelling. Many felt compelled to bury the victims, but the ground was icy and rock-solid.

With the rising number of deaths and lack of transport in the city, corpses could not be collected. Instead the inhabitants had to bring the dead to the cemeteries or morgues that were simply no more than dugouts. Throughout the early winter of 1942 the problem became much worse. The mounting numbers of bodies were lying in the streets or courtyards for many days, and an ever-growing parade of carts and sledges collected the dead through the main streets. A deathly silence had befallen the city except for the audible crump of German shelling. All public transportation had ceased, the streets were empty except for an occasional supply truck passing by and almost every factory was at a standstill. The city was said to resemble a ghost town rather than a place with almost 7 million inhabitants.

Although the Leningraders were resilient, resourceful people, the drastic shortages of all materials including proper warm clothing were killing more than 6,000 people each day. Men, women and children were collapsing and dying everywhere.

Out on the Leningrad Front Russian soldiers were also struggling to survive. 'One of the men from our battery has frozen feet,' wrote a Russian soldier, 'He is in hospital. Both his legs are being amputated. There are already 2,000 such cases … we must give each soldier two pairs of socks, or the cold will bring about our defeat.'

Although soldiers at the front were receiving more rations than the civilians, they too were starving. As a result, many soldiers were falling ill or becoming too exhausted to fight. To make matters worse, a large number of soldiers fighting on the Leningrad Front were native Leningraders themselves. Consequently, their morale was greatly affected by the fate of their loved ones besieged inside the city.

Civilians collecting water in a street during the winter of 1942. In January of that year energy supplies were destroyed by German bombardments of the city. Heating supplies were also destroyed, causing yet more deaths.

(**Opposite, above**) Leningrad defence troops can be seen here marching along a road, making their way out to the perimeter of the city.

(**Opposite, below**) A civilian is seen here collecting firewood from the remnants of a destroyed building in the city. With facilities destroyed, there was a worrying prospect that Leningraders would starve or freeze to death. However, between February and April 1942 bread rations were increased to 300g per child per day. Adult workers were allowed a ration of 500g per day. Frozen food was delivered in limited amounts only to support active soldiers and key industrial workers. Some food supplies were delivered across the ice on Lake Ladoga. However, many delivery cars were destroyed by enemy aircraft.

(**Above**) Russian troops can be seen here congregating along Moskovsky Prospekt on 7 December 1941. These troops would have been used to defend the city perimeter and assist in allowing supplies to get through.

Civilians are shown here grieving over their dead in the city streets. The total civilian death toll in the second year of the siege amounted to some 500,000 citizens. The deadliest months of the siege were January and February 1942 when some 130,000 civilians were found dead in Leningrad and its suburbs each month.

This photograph shows women looking for water under the icy ground. During the siege, winters were the time of the highest mortality rates among the civilian population. Tens of thousands froze to death in Leningrad.

Women are seen here collecting water from a broken water pipe in the street. Pipelines were constantly destroyed by German bombing.

(**Opposite**) Two photographs showing the 21cm Kanone 39 (K 39) that was used as part of the siege apparatus against the city of Leningrad. The K 39 and its variants served as mobile artillery only with Artillery Battalions (*Artillerie-Abteilungen*) 767 and 768, each battalion being organized into three batteries, each with two guns. These batteries were initially moved to Army Group South and participated in the sieges of Odessa and Sevastopol. However, 768 Artillery Battalion was then assigned to Army Group North to aid in the siege of Leningrad.

(**Above**) The first winter on the Eastern Front and soldiers can be seen here using animal draught to transport supplies on a sled from one part of the Leningrad Front to another. The troops are wearing the standard issue greatcoat with a toque and M1938 field cap. The German army lacked the provisions to sustain their forces for a winter war and many thousands of their men got frostbite and other ailments caused by the cold.

(**Above**) The barrel of a heavy mortar being transported in the snow by a dual-bogie carriage. For travel this heavy howitzer could be broken up into two separate components: one the barrel and the remainder the weapon.

(**Opposite, above**) Winter-clad Soviet reconnaissance troops near Pulkovo Heights can be seen here advancing on skis south of Leningrad in March 1942.

(**Opposite, below**) The first of four photographs showing artillery *truppen* preparing their gun for a heavy fire mission against a target and a heavy bombardment of the city perimeter during the winter of 1942.

Winter-clad Wehrmacht grenadiers wearing their reversible jackets white-side-out can be seen here occupying a captured Russian defensive position outside the city perimeter. Note the knocked-out Soviet tank turret.

(**Opposite, above**) A howitzer being fired at a Soviet position during a night-time attack. Note the artillery crew plugging their ears as the charge leaves the barrel.

(**Opposite, below**) German artillerymen can be seen here trudging along an icy road towards the front. Their supplies and equipment are being transported by animal draught.

(**Above**) A heavy German mortar being prepared for a fire mission. The crew is shown here posing for the camera while the gun was operating in battlefield conditions.

(**Opposite, above**) Russian troops are gathered around a camp fire preparing food during a lull in the fighting. Two of the soldiers are armed with the PPDD 1940 submachine gun. They are all wearing their greatcoats and *shapka-ushanka* caps.

(**Opposite, below**) Russian soldiers carrying a wounded comrade at Neva Dubrovka near Leningrad.

(**Above**) German troops are seen here erecting a makeshift shelter for their artillery. Such shelters offered no real protection for the crews other than providing the crew, their ammunition and the gun with some defence against the harsh Russian elements.

Soviet white-washed BA-10 fighting vehicles near Leningrad during winter operations, probably in 1943. The BA-10 was the most prolific Soviet heavy armoured car during the war on the Eastern Front. It was armed with a T-26/BT turret with a potent 45mm high-velocity gun.

Winter-clad Russian troops can be seen here assaulting an enemy position during operations probably in 1943. Often during an attack the infantry would be supported by heavy artillery in order to break through the enemy's forward positions, thus allowing the mobile troops to exploit the breach to penetrate the enemy's defensive positions and destroy rear support and service units. By 1943 Russian infantry units received substantial numbers of automatic weapons and supporting artillery.

At first glance this image looks like it depicts a trench being dug for the soldiers' protection; however, these are pioneers constructing a base for an artillery shelter.

(**Opposite**) Two photographs showing a howitzer positioned inside a newly-constructed shelter during the siege operation in 1942.

(**Above**) A heavy artillery crew poses for the camera with their elevated gun in a typical specially-constructed installation.

(**Opposite, above**) A captured French howitzer used as part of the siege ordnance against Russian positions on the outskirts of Leningrad during the summer of 1942.

(**Opposite, below**) An interesting photograph showing a 21cm crew preparing their weapon's barrel to be connected to the main firing platform. This was an enormous weapon that was transported in two pieces. For travel the barrel was manoeuvred onto a separate trailer. The carriage carried an integral firing platform that was lowered to the ground when emplacing the howitzer. The wheels were then cranked up off the ground and it was prepared for firing. Note the platform on the right of the picture.

(**Above**) An artilleryman posing for the camera on the integral firing platform next to the open gun tube during operations around Leningrad in the spring of 1942.

A 21cm Mörser 18 crew preparing their weapon for a fire mission. This weapon was used in independent battalions and heavy artillery batteries, but it was also used as coastal artillery due to its siege success around Leningrad. The firing procedure of this weapon consisted of feeding six charges into the gun tube to fire a single projectile. This gave the gun greater distance capability against enemy targets.

Wehrmacht soldiers are shown here using a support vehicle as cover as they assault an enemy position on the outskirts of Leningrad in 1942. Note the two MG 34 machine-gunners inside the rear of vehicle giving the attacking troops additional fire-power support.

An 8.8cm flak gun being readied for action by a shirtless crew member. This was the most famous German anti-aircraft gun of the Second World War. The gun was bolted onto a cruciform platform from which it fired with outriggers extended. As the Soviet Air Force gradually grew in size and began inflicting ever-greater casualties on German positions, so grew the need for more 8.8cm flak guns to try to counter the growing threat.

Four photographs showing the destruction of Leningrad by heavy German bombardments. Hundreds of Luftwaffe bombers constantly made a series of heavy air-raids on Leningrad with incendiary and high-explosive bombs. During the course of the whole siege an estimated 75,000 bombs were dropped on the city, killing 50,000 civilians and destroying thousands of homes and commercial buildings.

(**Above**) Civilians pass one of the many buildings destroyed in Leningrad by both German ground and aerial attacks.

(**Opposite, above**) A dead loved one wrapped in blankets and tied up for burial is shown here being hauled along a street on a makeshift flat-bed trolley. Children look on at the spectacle. Although part of the civilian population was evacuated from Leningrad during the siege, many died while trying to escape. Thousands of people died in various air-raids and from starvation and cold while trying to leave the city. Most bodies were never buried due to the constant bombing and other attacks by German forces.

(**Opposite, below**) The dead are shown here being collected from the road and put on the back of a transport vehicle. Thousands of civilians were by now being slowly starved to death and often collapsed in the road while looking for food. As starvation gripped Leningraders, in desperation some began killing and eating zoo animals and household pets. People were so hungry that many began to strip the walls of rooms, removing the paste and boiling it to make soup. Even old leather was boiled and eaten in order to stay alive. The extreme hunger drove some to eat the corpses of the dead who had been largely preserved by the sub-zero temperatures.

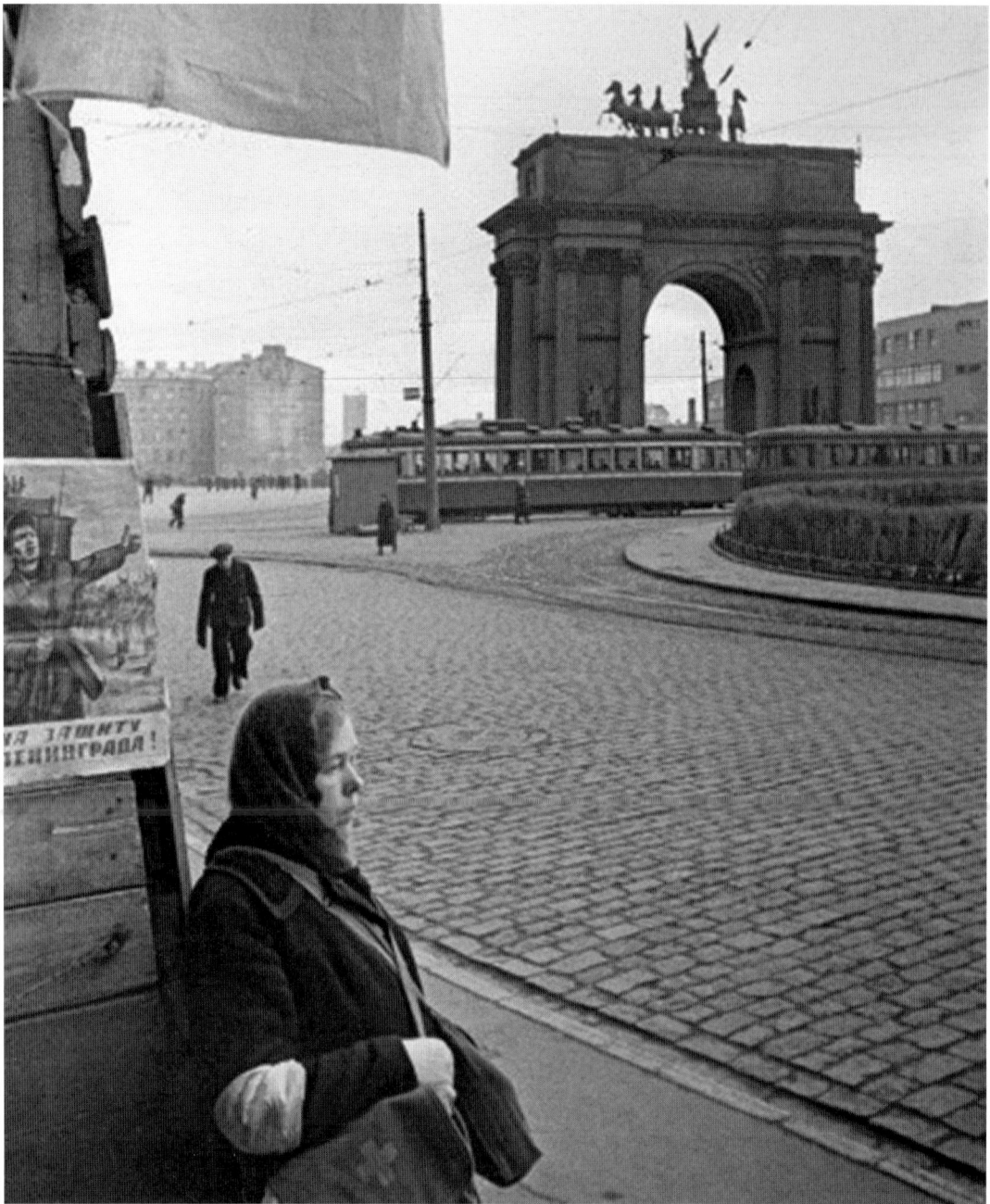

(**Above**) A Russian civilian at a first-aid post near the Narva Triumphal Arch inside the city.

(**Opposite, above**) A group of Leningrad defence troops poses for the camera after retrieving an unexploded German shell in a street. This was one of the most efficient large high-explosive shells used against the city. These projectiles were designed for bunker-busting and for use against other well-defended reinforced positions. However, hundreds of them were directed against innocent civilians.

(**Opposite, below**) In spite of the heavy bombing and extensive damage of the city, Leningraders tried their best to survive and live life as normally as possible. In this photograph civilians can be seen walking along a decimated street.

(**Opposite, above**) Some civilians are seen here retrieving what belongings they could from their burning house following a heavy enemy artillery bombardment. After heavy German bombing many houses and warehouses were burned and destroyed by massive fires. Huge amounts of stored food reserves such as grain, flour and sugar as well as other food supplies were completely destroyed in both ground and aerial bombardments.

(**Opposite, below**) Dead Leningraders can be seen here lying on the pavement. Many of them died of either starvation or illness. In early 1942 the first cases of cholera were registered in Leningrad. By March the infection was isolated and then stopped. Although an epidemic was prevented, hospitals were suffering from severe bombing, shortages of energy and lack of food. Thousands of doctors and nurses were killed at work.

(**Above**) A common scene inside the city was dead loved ones being wrapped in white cloth and transported by sledge for their burial.

A large bomb crater filled with water being pumped out into the River Neva.

A Soviet KV-1 tank on parade at the Palace Square in Leningrad, 1 May 1942, celebrating Workers' Day.

(**Opposite**) Kolomna cabbages being grown in front of St Isaac's Cathedral. The food shortages had become so acute between 1941 and 1942 that by the summer of 1942 starvation-level rationing was eased by new vegetable gardens that covered most open patches of ground in the city.

(**Above**) An interesting photograph taken in September 1942 showing battle boats arriving at Leningrad via Lake Ladoga. They were transporting vital food and supplies to the city.

Chapter Four

The 'Ice Road'

Amid the destruction of the German blockade, all hopes of supplying the inhabitants of the city and the Soviets units defending its outskirts were not lost. Since November 1941 Lake Ladoga had been frozen, enabling urgent supplies to be transported across the frozen lake by wheeled vehicles into Leningrad. Lieutenant General Zakhar Kondratyev, who was the head of the Main Administration of the Red Army Road Transport and Road Service, wrote:

> They built access roads, cut down wood for supplies, erected warehouses and bases, various kinds of buildings for heating, food, medical and technical aid stations. We prepared road signs, landmarks, portable shields and bridges, in case of cracks on ice. Auto repair shops, telegraph and telephone stations were equipped and camouflage equipment was prepared. Similar work was being done on the eastern shore of the lake. More than 300 traffic controllers, mostly women, stood along the 'Road of Life', dressed all in white with flags and flashlights. These 'White Angels', as they were called, were highly visible not only to Soviet drivers, but also to enemy snipers and pilots.

The city was to owe its whole existence and survival to what became known to the Russians as the 'life road' or the 'ice road'. This perilous route stretched from the towns of Kabona and Lednevo. From here the freight trains would take supplies into the city and leave carrying hundreds of civilians to safety. Many thousands of evacuees often did not wait for transport and made the hazardous trip on foot, crossing the lake out of the pocket between 6 December 1941 and 22 January 1942. A large-scale civilian evacuation, mainly of those who were unable to work such as women, children and the infirm, were transported out in late January 1942. Some 554,000 civilians were evacuated from 22 January to 15 April 1942. Wounded soldiers were also evacuated. Some 35,000 soldiers were removed from the city. Industrial equipment from eighty-six plants and factories and some art and museum collections were also removed at the beginning of December 1941.

Although thousands of tons of vital supplies reached the city and many thousands of troops and civilians were evacuated, it had been a very dangerous operation with the loss of many support vehicles. Not only was the convoy of trucks attacked by the

Luftwaffe and shelled by Finnish and German artillery, but the 'ice road' itself was hazardous. The continuing blizzards, the depth of the snow that sometimes halted traffic for several days or more and freezing arctic temperatures caused many vehicles to become trapped or engines to fail. For many miles the road was littered with more than 300 trucks at any one time that had been blown up or had broken down, while others had fallen into shell holes.

Initially supply into the city via the 'ice road' was slow and laborious. However, slowly through the winter of 1942 the operation improved, reaching its peak performance in March. By the spring the supply line received additional reinforcements. Lieutenant General Andrey Kozlov recollected: 'On 22 and 23 April 1942, about eleven thousand soldiers with weapons were transferred to the eastern shore through Ladoga – reinforcement for the 54th Army. Only half of the way across by cars, the other half was on foot in icy water.'

During the later stages of the relief operation there were more than 400 3-ton trucks moving on the road each day. To help speed up the flow of supplies, hundreds of vehicles throughout Russia were hastily sent to the area. German positions some 13 miles away continued to bombard the 'ice road', but were unable to shell with sufficient intensity. A German commander grudgingly noted: 'In view of the great distance from the German lines [to the ice road] there is little expectation that artillery fire can produce appreciable pressure on the Russians.' The 'ice road' had inevitably thwarted German plans to starve the city to death, despite it being continually attacked by aircraft and artillery. Various attempts were made by the Germans to target individual areas of the 'ice road' in order to try to break it up, but failed due to the vastness of the area.

Despite the fact that the Russians were unable to lift the blockade of Leningrad completely, the city had finally been liberated by a corridor of ice that established a direct link to a starving location. In total some 356,000 tons of supplies were transported, including 271,000 tons of food, 32,000 tons of military supplies and 37,000 tons of fuel. In April 1942 the State Defence Committee ordered the Red Army to construct a pipeline that entered service weeks later on 18 June. This pipeline was 30 miles long and 8 miles deep and delivered 295 tonnes of fuel per day. Electricity was also later restored to the city via underwater cables.

The success of the 'ice road' saw the Russians building new ice roads during the winter of 1942–43. The roads opened on 19 December and the first convoy of trucks crossed the next day. The roads were serviceable for 101 days between 20 December 1942 and 30 March 1943. Some 210,000 tonnes of supplies were fed into Leningrad in that time, mainly comprising food and ammunition, with more than 200,000 personnel also being evacuated from the city.

The 'ice road', or the 'road of life' as the Leningraders referred to it, was a transport route built on ice to move important equipment and supplies across Lake Ladoga into Leningrad. This frozen surface provided the only winter 'roads' into the city and they operated in the winters of 1941/42 and 1942/43. Pioneers and soldiers constructed and operated these routes under perilous conditions, often being bombarded by both ground and aerial attacks.

Supplies being moved on sled by animal draught across the ice. These supplies were essential to sustain life and resistance inside the Leningrad pocket. The 'ice road' was also used to evacuate non-combatants, the wounded and industrial equipment. During its operation more than 1.3 million people, principally women and children, were evacuated over the roads during the siege.

(**Above**) Winter-clad Wehrmacht anti-tank gunners next to their whitewashed PaK35/36. The Germans often set up various positions in order to try to block or hinder supplies being fed into the city. These PaK guns were powerful enough to knock out supply vehicles or infantry transport lorries.

(**Opposite**) A Russian 'female regulator' overseeing supplies being moved across the 'ice road' into the city. The road first opened in November 1941, but truck losses carrying supplies were huge. On many occasions wheeled vehicles became stuck in snowdrifts and were frequently abandoned after their drivers became lost. Some sank into the ice where the Germans had been pounding parts of the road with artillery fire.

(**Below**) A number of trucks can be seen here on the 'ice road', precariously making their way back and forth to the city. It was initially reckoned that some 1,965 tonnes of supplies were required each day to feed Leningrad, but at first this could not be achieved. During the initial stages of the 'ice road' operation some 1,300 out of 3,500 trucks were put out of service with a staggering 1,004 lost altogether.

(**Opposite, above**) A column of supply trucks making their way across the 'ice road' during an early-morning operation. By the end of December the 'ice road' was 1 metre thick and covered with 30 centimetres of snow. This meant that supplies were able to cross the road with unlimited numbers of vehicles including heavy trucks as well.

(**Opposite, below**) A Russian 'regulator' directing traffic across the 'ice road'. From late December 1941 until February 1942 the Leningrad pocket received massive amounts of supplies. This enabled not only sustaining the troops fighting at the front but beginning to help the civilians who were starving to death.

(**Above**) Wheeled transport: an animal draught can be seen here moving supplies onto the 'ice road'. Between February and March 1942 the Russians were able to deliver more than four times the quantity of supplies they had initially achieved between November and December 1941.

Civilians and industrial apparatus are being evacuated from the city via the 'ice road'. On Stalin's orders industrial evacuation was the most important task when the roads first opened. However, he was also mindful that the evacuation of civilians was another priority, including wounded and sick soldiers. Some 554,000 civilians were evacuated between 22 January and 15 April 1942.

Two photographs showing a German 21cm Mörser preparing for a fire mission. Often these howitzers were used to bombard the 'ice road' in order to try to weaken the ice and prevent supplies from entering the Leningrad pocket.

(**Above**) Pioneers are seen here constructing a wooden frame in order to allow heavy traffic to pass across weakened parts of the 'ice road' during the winter thaw.

(**Opposite, above**) A female 'regulator' directing the traffic onto the 'ice road'. Note her white flag that was used in order to instruct traffic to pass and stop. This was undertaken to ensure traffic moving at intervals due to the weight loading on the ice. The 'regulator' was also used to halt traffic during a suspected artillery or aerial bombardment of the road.

(**Opposite, below**) Here a KV-1 tank has evidently fallen through the ice and troops are attempting to hoist it out with rigging. Often, especially during the initial stages of the winter of 1941, the Russians evacuated a number of military vehicles from the pocket and transported them eastwards to take up new positions.

(**Opposite**) Another photograph of a 'regulator' directing traffic along the 'ice road' using their white flag.

(**Above**) Due to the constant dangers involved in making air drops of supplies over the city, Russian aircraft often landed near Lake Ladoga and unloaded their cargo of supplies for the waiting trucks. In this photograph an aircraft unloads its supplies onto a truck that was then driven across the 'ice road' into the Leningrad pocket.

Chapter Five

The Turning-Point

In spite of the success of the 'ice road', with the spring thaw approaching the Germans were determined to prevent any supplies from getting into the city. However, Hitler himself wanted to capture Leningrad, but only after success in the Crimea and Caucasus. Yet in spite of this, the plan was drawn up and named Operation NORTHERN LIGHT or Operation *NORDLICHT*. It was for a massive attack across the Neva River in order to make contact with the Finns east of Leningrad, thereby establishing a closed ring around the city. Once Leningrad was surrounded, an all-out assault was planned that included simultaneously bombarding the city by aerial attacks and using more than 800 artillery pieces.

The bold offensive was scheduled to be launched against the city on 23 August 1942. However, Soviet command had already detected large German movements and a considerable build-up of forces on the Leningrad Front. This prompted the Russian 2nd Shock and 8th Armies to take the initiative on 27 August and launch their own massive offensive in the Siniavino-Mga sector and at Tosno and Uritsk. For four weeks German soldiers fought a series of heavy unrelenting bloody battles to hold their positions around Leningrad. The Germans immediately launched a counter-offensive that saw the first deployment of the new Tiger tanks, but these made only limited gains against overwhelming enemy attacks. Although strong German units held grimly to their lines and managed to blunt Russian penetrations, the losses were immense. The battle had absorbed all the available resources of the 18th Army and elements of the 11th, consequently resulting in the planned assault on Leningrad being abandoned. A German soldier who had spent weeks fighting on the Leningrad Front wrote:

Nothing could have possibly prepared us for the hell we endured in front of Leningrad. Our commander gave us boys all hope that this slaughter would be over by autumn. Already we have lost hundreds of comrades. I have seen my comrades killed and ripped to pieces by the Russian attacks. Whole groups of them were either blasted into oblivion or forced to retreat. Often in the terrible confusion many soldiers ran the wrong way, only to be mown down or captured and tortured to death.

For the German forces dug in around Leningrad, a cruel frustration now gripped them with a sense of futility and gloom. Already thousands of their comrades had been killed, and by mid-October 1942 they found themselves substantially in the same position as in the spring of that year. Because of the defeats in southern Russia, German forces were now compelled to go over to the offensive against growing resistance. Despite the prevailing conditions and the daily shelling, Leningrad itself gradually regained strength and became a strong fortress capable of withstanding a further year and a half of siege.

It now seemed that the heroic and tragic period of the siege had finally come to an end. Although war-weary, the Leningraders were inspired by their resilience and energy to prevail over a terrible situation. Irrepressible as ever, the military council began their winter defence training and arming more than 300,000 Leningraders into self-defence groups. Everyone between the ages of 14 and 60 was required to carry out civil defence duties in the city.

At last, following the deaths of more than 1 million people, Leningrad had finally become a fortress city and was prepared to play a decisive role in Soviet strategy. Although the defence had been costly and somewhat futile, it had managed to pin down huge parts of German Army Group North that had been needed elsewhere to prop up the other crumbling fronts.

When news of the Red Army's breakthrough finally came on 18 January 1943, it was greeted with joy in the city with numerous celebrations. Although life in Leningrad in 1943 would continue to be both hard and dangerous with frequent bombardments and heavy air attacks, Hitler's hopes and dreams of wiping Leningrad and its people off the face of the earth had failed, together with his invasion of Russia.

The siege continued until 27 January 1944 when the Russians unleashed the Leningrad-Novgorod offensive. It was an attack against the German Army Group North by the Soviet Volkhov and Leningrad Fronts along with elements of the 2nd Baltic Front. Its main objective was to fully lift the siege of Leningrad.

The Russians launched their offensive from the Novgorod area towards Luga against a part of the 18th Army. The German 18th Army was outnumbered by at least 3:1 in divisions, 3:1 in artillery and 6:1 in tanks, self-propelled artillery and aircraft. Although heavy losses were sustained by the 18th Army, it still was not entirely destroyed. However, their positions around Leningrad were lost forever and were reluctantly driven westwards by overwhelming enemy forces.

With Leningrad now relieved from its long siege, it was left to restore itself after 872 days of heavy bombing coupled with extreme famine, the disruption of utilities, water, energy and food supplies. The siege of Leningrad was one of the most barbaric sieges in world history. It was undoubtedly a racially-motivated starvation policy by Hitler that was an integral part of his aim to exterminate the population of the Soviet Union.

Out on patrol and German infantry wearing the two-piece snow suit and their steel helmets have received an application of whitewash for camouflage. While the reversible 'white-side-out' garment provided the soldiers with adequate winter camouflage, it often became soiled with mud and grime and as a consequence became more conspicuous against the winter background.

Setting up a position with a howitzer near Krasny Bor are soldiers of the Spanish Blue Division. In August 1942, the Blue Division was transferred north to the south-eastern flank for operations around Leningrad, just south of the River Neva near Pushkin, Kolpino and Krasny Bor in the River Izhora area. The Blue Division faced a major Soviet attempt to break the siege of Leningrad in February 1943 when the Soviet 55th Army attacked Spanish positions at the Battle of Krasny Bor near the main Moscow-Leningrad road.

(**Opposite, above**) A Wehrmacht 10.5cm le.FH.18/42 infantry gun crew preparing their weapon for a fire mission. The 10.5cm gun was the standard light artillery piece deployed in the divisions on the Eastern Front. However, in order to give the gun better punch on the battlefield, the weapon was modified in 1942. The barrel was lengthened, a cage muzzle brake was fitted and the carriage was a lightened version of the le.FH.18 design. Throughout the war the 10.5cm gun provided both the Wehrmacht and the Waffen-SS with a versatile and relatively mobile base of fire.

(**Opposite, below**) A field hospital along the Soviet Volkhov Front near Leningrad during winter operations in early 1943.

(**Above**) A staged Russian propaganda image showing Soviet troops heroically charging an enemy position near Leningrad in early 1943.

(**Above**) Soviet troops of the Leningrad and Volkhov Fronts meeting near Leningrad on 18 January 1943. The Volkhov Front's 372nd Rifle Division met troops of the 123rd Rifle Brigade of the Leningrad Front, opening an 8-mile-wide land corridor that could provide some relief to the besieged population of Leningrad. The Soviets then quickly constructed a railway line through the corridor which allowed more supplies to reach the city than via the 'road of life' across the frozen surface of Lake Ladoga. This corridor and the troops defending it meant reducing the possibilities of the capture of Leningrad and of any German-Finnish link-up.

(**Opposite, above**) A Soviet 85mm M1939 (52-K) anti-aircraft gun defending the skies inside the city. This powerful anti-aircraft weapon was used extensively against German aerial attacks on Leningrad during the siege. Sometimes the crews utilized the gun in an anti-tank role as well.

(**Opposite, below**) German troops passing a bomb crater full of water. The extent of the devastation can be seen following heavy fighting in the area. On 18 January 1943, the Red Army went on the offensive in order to try smashing the siege of Leningrad and driving back the forces of Army Group North. Although the Soviet attack went well, the German defensive positions were still too powerful as they had built strong fortifications to the south of Lake Ladoga.

(**Above**) Soviet defence soldiers on exercise in front of Leningrad.

(**Opposite, above**) A German flame-thrower burns a house during its unit's withdrawal from a position in the spring of 1943. During this period the Russians attempted to decisively defeat Army Group North and to lift the siege altogether. However, success was limited and German defences along with their scorched-earth policy hindered the Russian attacks. Yet Soviet forces still made a number of other attempts throughout 1943 to renew their offensive and to lift the siege completely, but achieved only minor successes.

(**Opposite, below**) Spanish infantry moving forward during an enemy contact around Leningrad in the summer of 1943. The Spaniards were able to hold significant ground against strong Russian attacks that were a number of times greater than them. As a result they contained the Soviet advances and the siege of Leningrad was maintained for a further year. The division remained on the Leningrad Front where it continued to suffer heavy casualties due to the weather and constant enemy contact.

(**Above**) From the River Volkhov to the Gulf of Finland the German Front was reminiscent of the First World War, with a string of trenches and shell holes in which gains and losses could be measured only in yards.

(**Opposite, above**) A German PaK crew during a lull in the fighting. By the summer of 1943, the front continued to hold. The German strength in July was 710,000 men, and German forces were also building up a huge number of reserves echeloned in depth behind the northern fronts in Estonia and Latvia. The Germans and the Soviets in northern Russia were almost equal in strength, but the Red Army was known to have substantial reserves. They were also building up significant forces to weaken Army Group North's defensive positions around Leningrad and Nevel.

(**Opposite, below**) Supplies for Leningrad being unloaded from a barge on Lake Ladoga and moved on a narrow-gauge train.

An anti-aircraft gun crew firing at enemy planes during a defensive action in Leningrad.

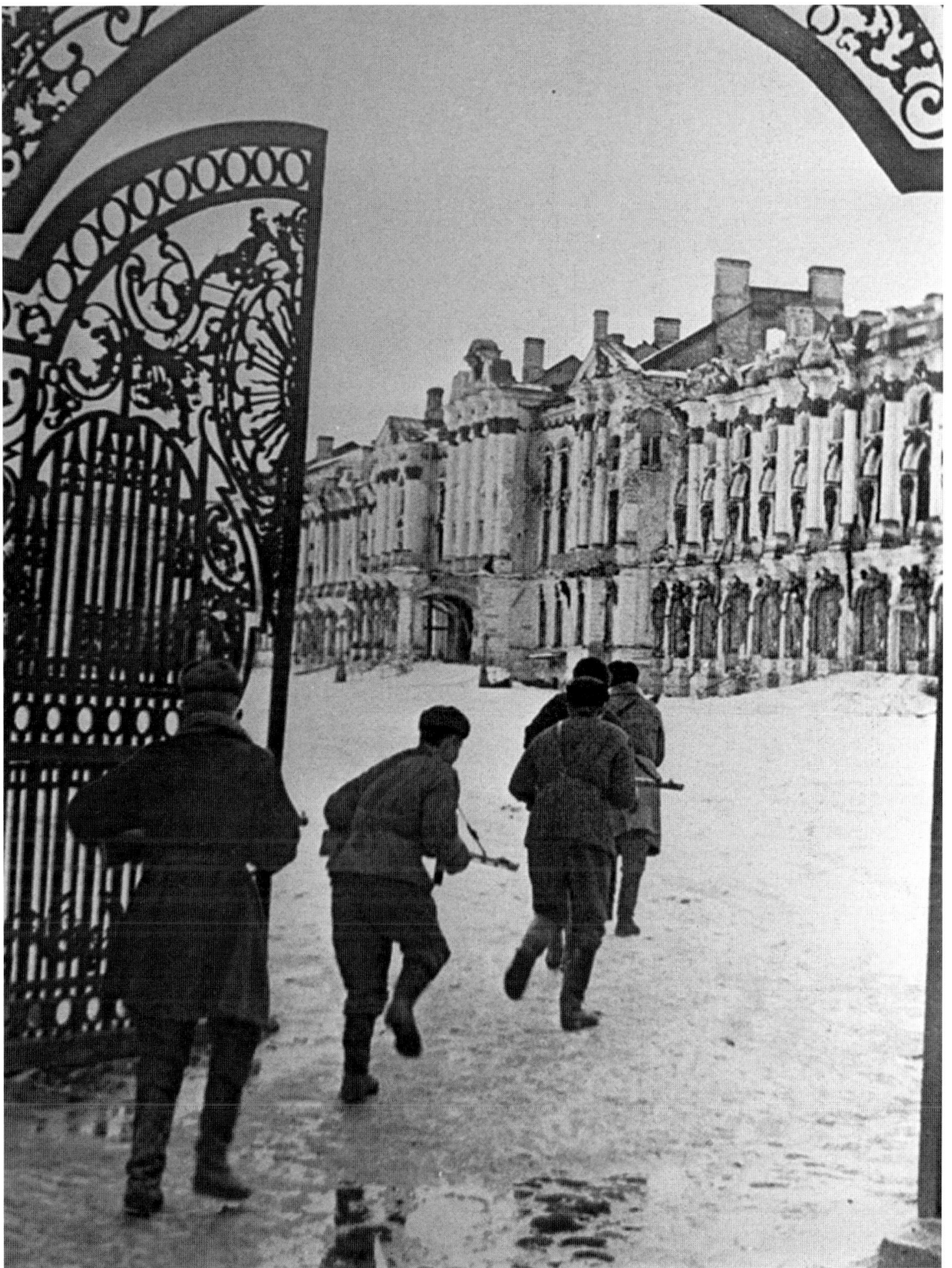

Soviet troops can be seen here fighting in the Pushkin district of Leningrad in early 1944.

(**Opposite, above**) A night-time Russian artillery barrage in early 1944. The battery consists of Russian 152mm ML-20 howitzer Model 1937 guns.

(**Opposite, below**) An 8.8cm flak gun complete with a *Schützschild* (splinter shield) being used against ground targets. The Russians launched their winter offensive against the Leningrad and Volkhov Fronts on 14 January 1944. In some sectors along the front some units barely had enough Panzers to oppose the Russian armour and called upon flak battalions to halt the Red Army's attacks. The German 18th Army was outnumbered by at least 3:1 in divisions, 3:1 in artillery and 6:1 in tanks, self-propelled artillery and aircraft. By the morning of 18 January the fronts east of Oranienbaum and west of Leningrad were collapsing.

(**Above**) During the Russian Leningrad and Volkhov offensive *Nebelwerfer truppen* can be seen here with their projectiles preparing the barrelled rocket-launcher to be fired against an enemy target. This weapon fired 2.5kg shells that could be projected over a range of 7,000 metres. When fired the projectiles screamed through the air, causing the enemy to become unnerved by the noise. These fearsome weapons caused extensive carnage along the Russian Front. They served in independent army rocket-launcher battalions and later in the war in regiments and brigades.

Red Army soldiers celebrating the end of the siege of Leningrad on 27 January 1944.

A Soviet soldier being awarded the Defence of Leningrad medal on 1 June 1944.

Chapter Six

The Outcome

Now that Leningrad was relieved, by 18 January the fronts east of Oranienbaum and west of Leningrad quickly began to collapse. The same was happening at Novgorod where a number of German units were being encircled. The Russian Second Shock and 42nd Armies then joined the attack against German divisions in front of Leningrad. The Soviet attacks were so furious that the bulk of German force withdrew along the Baltic Coast. Many were trapped and destroyed as the Russians swept in from the east and west. As the German Front west of Leningrad caved in, the Russians continued to make gains. The 18th Army was beginning to disintegrate. Fighting in mud and swampland, the troops were exhausted. On 23 January Pushkin and Slutsk were evacuated. Despite appeals by commanders in the field to withdraw, Hitler responded angrily and prohibited all voluntary withdrawals. However, one week later, after the 18th Army had incurred more than 50,000 casualties, Hitler approved a retreat to the River Luga but directed that the front be held, contact with the 16th Army regained and all gaps in the front closed.

On 2 February 1944, the Red Army launched a series of heavy attacks and was soon within reach of the frontier of Estonia. Two weeks later troops of the Volkhov Front, as well as the 42nd and 67th Armies of the Leningrad Front, reached Lake Peipus. On 18 February, Soviet troops of the 2nd Baltic Front carried out large-scale attacks with parts of the Leningrad Front against the German 16th Army of Army Group North with the aim of liberating vast areas south-west of Lake Ilmen. As a result of the operation, Russian forces drove out the Germans and chased the retreating forces 160 miles to the west, liberating cities and towns as they advanced.

The German withdrawal from Leningrad had consequently caused a chain reaction of defeats for German Army Group North, from which they were never to recover. Many of the German divisions had spent more than two years dug in around the city and had not been given additional reinforcements with which to defend themselves against a potential large-scale enemy offensive. Much of their time had been spent in bombing Leningrad and preventing Soviet forces supplying the starving city.

When the Red Army finally launched their major winter offensive in January 1944, Army Group North was ill-equipped and under strength. Within weeks of Leningrad being relieved from its long siege, the bulk of the German forces had been driven out of the Soviet Union and were defending the frontiers of Estonia and Lithuania.

Appendix I

German Order of Battle

Army Group North

(Field Marshal Wilhelm Ritter von Leeb)

8 August 1941

18th Army (*Generaloberst* Georg von Küchler)
(The XXXXII Army Corps was transferred to the 18th Army on 18 July 1941.)
XXXXII Army Corps (Walter Kuntze)
    61st Infantry Division   217th Infantry Division
XXVI Army Corps (Albert Wodrig)
    93rd Infantry Division   291st Infantry Division
    254th Infantry Division

Panzergruppe 4 (*Generaloberst* Erich Hoepner)
XXXXI Corps (mot.) (Georg-Hans Reinhardt)
    1st Infantry Division   8th Panzer Division
    1st Panzer Division   36th Infantry Division (mot.)
    6th Panzer Division
LVI Motorized Corps (Erich von Manstein)
    269th Infantry Division   3rd Infantry Division (mot.)
    SS *Polizei* Division
XXXVIII Corps (Friedrich-Wilhelm von Chappuis)
    58th Infantry Division
L Army Corps (Georg Lindemann) (from 14 August 1941)
    269th Infantry Division   SS *Polizei* Division

16th Army (*Generaloberst* Ernst Busch)
XXVIII Army Corps (Mauritz von Wiktorin)
    96th Infantry Division   122nd Infantry Division
    121st Infantry Division   SS *Totenkopf* Division
I Army Corps (Kuno-Hans von Both)
    11th Infantry Division   126th Infantry Division
    21st Infantry Division

II Army Corps (Walter von Brockdorff-Ahlefeldt)
    12th Infantry Division   123rd Infantry Division
    32nd Infantry Division
X Army Corps (Christian Hansen)
    30th Infantry Division   290th Infantry Division

3rd Panzer Group

XXXIX Motorized Corps (Rudolf Schmidt)
    12th Panzer Division   20th Motorized Division
    18th Motorized Division
LVII Motorized Corps (Adolf-Friedrich Kuntzen)
    19th Panzer Division   20th Panzer Division

Luftflotte 1 (3 August 1941)

2.(F)/ObdL Wekusta (2nd Squadron, Long-Range Reconnaissance Luftwaffe High Command)
1 KGr z.b.V. 106 (1st Transport Squadron, 106th Military Transport Group)

I. *Fliegerkorps*

5th Squadron, 122nd Intelligence Group
Kampfgeschwader 1: He 111H, Ju 88A (Group 2 and 3)
Kampfgeschwader 76: Ju 88A
Kampfgeschwader 77: Ju 88A
Sturzkampfgeschwader 77: Ju 87B, Bf 110
Zerstörergeschwader 26: Bf 110 (Group 1 and 2)
Jagdgeschwader 54: Bf 109F
Jagdgeschwader 53: Bf 109F (Group 2 only)

VIII. *Fliegerkorps*

(The *VIII. Fliegerkorps* took part in the operation from late July to 20 September 1941.)
2nd Squadron, 11th Intelligence Group
1st Transport Squadron, 4th Transport Group
Kampfgeschwader 2: Do 17Z (Group 1)
Kampfgeschwader 3: Do 17Z (Group 3)
Schnellkampfgeschwader 210: Bf 110 (Group 2)
Sturzkampfgeschwader 2: Ju 87B (Group 1 and 3)
Lehrgeschwader 2: Bf 109E, Hs-123 (2nd and 10th Squadrons)
Jagdgeschwader 27: Bf 109F, Bf 109E (Group 3 only)
Jagdgeschwader 52: Bf 109F (Group 2 only)

Red Army Order of Battle

Northern Front Defensive Operations
10 July to 23 August 1941

The Northern Fronts were divided into the Karelian and Leningrad Fronts.

1 July 1941

23rd Army (defending the approaches north of Leningrad)

16th Rifle Division	39th Fighter Aviation Division
70th Rifle Division	41st Bomber Aviation Division
177th Rifle Division	1st Mixed Aviation Division
191st Rifle Division	2nd Mixed Aviation Division
1st Mountain Rifle Brigade	3rd Mixed Aviation Division
8th Rifle Brigade	4th Mixed Aviation Division
Separate Kursantska Rifle Brigade	5th Mixed Aviation Division
21st Fortified Region	55th Mixed Aviation Division
22nd Fortified Region	3rd PVO Fighter Aviation Division
12th Engineer Regiment	54th PVO Fighter Aviation Division
29th Engineer Regiment	14th Bomber Aviation Regiment

1 August 1941

11th Army	110th High-Power Howitzer Artillery Regiment
27th Army	
Novgorod Operational Group	402nd High-Power Howitzer Artillery Regiment
5th Airborne Corps	
9th Airborne Brigade	429th High-Power Howitzer Artillery Regiment (RVGK)
10th Airborne Brigade	
201st Airborne Brigade	11th Anti-Aircraft Artillery Battalion
41st Cavalry Division (forming)	19th Anti-Aircraft Artillery Battalion
9th Anti-Tank Brigade	10th PVO Brigade
10th Anti-Tank Brigade	Riga PVO Brigade Region
270th Corps Artillery Regiment	Estonian PVO Brigade Region
448th Corps Artillery Regiment	Kaunas PVO Brigade Region

1st Mechanized Corps
3rd Tank Division
12th Mechanized Corps
23rd Tank Division
28th Tank Division
125th Tank Regiment
25th Engineer Battalion
110th Motorized Engineer Battalion

50th Pontoon-Bridge Battalion
55th Pontoon-Bridge Battalion
56th Pontoon-Bridge Battalion
57th Pontoon-Bridge Battalion
4th Mixed Aviation Division
6th Mixed Aviation Division
57th Mixed Aviation Division

1 September 1941

11th Army
27th Army
34th Army
Novgorod Operational Group
33rd Rifle Division
84th Rifle Division
54th Cavalry Division
310th Rifle Division (under command
   of the north-western direction)
10th Anti-Tank Brigade
402nd High-Power Howitzer Artillery
   Regiment (RVGK)
429th High-Power Howitzer Artillery
   Regiment (RVGK)
171st Anti-Tank Artillery Regiment
759th Anti-Tank Artillery Regiment

19th Anti-Aircraft Artillery Battalion
111th Anti-Aircraft Artillery Battalion
239th Anti-Aircraft Artillery Battalion
246th Anti-Aircraft Artillery Battalion
250th Anti-Aircraft Artillery Battalion
Riga PVO Brigade Region
Estonian PVO Brigade Region
Kaunas PVO Brigade Region
34th Motorcycle Regiment
25th Engineer Battalion
50th Pontoon-Bridge Battalion
55th Pontoon-Bridge Battalion
56th Pontoon-Bridge Battalion
57th Pontoon-Bridge Battalion
6th Mixed Aviation Division
415th Fighter Aviation Regiment

1 October 1941

11th Army
27th Army
34th Army
Novgorod Operational Group
25th Cavalry Division
46th Cavalry Division
54th Cavalry Division
10th Anti-Tank Brigade
171st Anti-Tank Artillery Regiment
759th Anti-Tank Artillery Regiment
3rd Guards Mortar Regiment
Riga PVO Brigade Region

Estonian PVO Brigade Region
Kaunas PVO Brigade Region
11th Anti-Aircraft Artillery Battalion
29th Anti-Aircraft Artillery Battalion
239th Anti-Aircraft Artillery Battalion
246th Anti-Aircraft Artillery Battalion
250th Anti-Aircraft Artillery Battalion
125th Tank Brigade
87th Tank Battalion
110th Tank Battalion
112th Tank Battalion
112th Tank Battalion

116th Tank Battalion
34th Motorcycle Regiment
57th Pontoon-Bridge Battalion
67th Sapper Battalion

492nd Sapper Battalion
494th Sapper Battalion
6th Mixed Aviation Division

Luga Operational Group/Southern Operational Group (1 August 1941)

41st Rifle Corps
111th Rifle Division
177th Rifle Division
235th Rifle Division
1st Rifle Regiment (3rd Leningrad
   People's Militia Division)
260th Machine-Gun Artillery Battalion

262nd Machine-Gun Artillery Battalion
541st Howitzer Artillery Regiment
   (RVGK)
Luga PVO Brigade Region
24th Tank Division
259th Sapper Battalion

Kopor Operational Group (1 September 1941)

1st Guards Leningrad People's Militia
   Division
2nd Leningrad People's Militia Division
522nd Rifle Regiment (191st Rifle
   Division)

519th Howitzer Artillery Regiment
   (RVGK)
24th Tank Regiment (1st Tank Division)
295th Sapper Battalion

Neva Operational Group (1 October 1941)

115th Rifle Division
1st Rifle Division (NKVD)
4th Naval Infantry Brigade
1st Fighter Battalion
4th Fighter Battalion
5th Fighter Battalion
230th Artillery Regiment (71st Rifle Division)

1/577th Howitzer Artillery Regiment
24th Anti-Tank Artillery Battalion
20th Mortar Battalion
107th Tank Battalion
21st Pontoon-Bridge Battalion

Novgorod Operational Group (1 August 1941)

16th Rifle Corps (headquarters used
   to form the 48th Army on 7 August)
70th Rifle Division
128th Rifle Division
237th Rifle Division
1st Leningrad People's Militia Division
1st Mountain Rifle Brigade
21st Tank Division
1 September 1941
305th Rifle Division
448th Corps Artillery Regiment

Separate Mortar Battalion
8th Anti-Aircraft Artillery Battalion
3rd Tank Division
28th Tank Division
50th Engineer Battalion
October 1941
180th Rifle Division
185th Rifle Division
305th Rifle Division
Mixed Rifle Regiment
264th Corps Artillery Regiment

448th Corps Artillery Regiment
Mortar Battalion (unnumbered)
8th Anti-Aircraft Battalion
242nd Anti-Aircraft Battalion
3rd Tank Division

25th Engineer Battalion
50th Engineer-Bridge Battalion
55th Engineer-Bridge Battalion
56th Engineer-Bridge Battalion